Marketing Plan for Business Growth

Acquire New Customers, Boost Profits, and Standing Tall in the Crowd

Lane J. Taylor

Table of contents

Introduction

In the fast-paced world of business, where competition is fierce and innovation is relentless, your success as an entrepreneur or business leader depends on more than just a great product or service. It hinges on your ability to navigate the intricate landscape of marketing. In today's dynamic marketplaces, having a comprehensive and effective marketing plan isn't just a choice; it's the lifeline that can help your business thrive and emerge as a shining star in a crowded constellation.

Welcome to "Marketing Plan for Business Growth: Acquire New Customers, Boost

Profits, and Standing Tall in the Crowd." Within these pages, we embark on an exhilarating journey through the realms of marketing strategy, customer acquisition, and profit optimization. This book isn't just a passive read; it's a roadmap that, when followed diligently, can transform your business trajectory.

As you venture forth, envision your business not as a static entity but as a dynamic force that can influence and innovate. Your business is not merely an offering in a marketplace; it is a story waiting to be told, a solution yearning to be discovered, and an experience that can change lives. And for this narrative to resonate, you must be a master of marketing.

You will traverse the marketing landscape, uncovering the secrets that drive customer engagement, brand loyalty, and sustainable growth. This journey begins by setting our destination, marked by crystal-clear objectives. The compass of a marketing plan points to where you want your business to be – perhaps acquiring new customers, boosting profits, or asserting a commanding presence in your industry. But to get there, you need a plan, and not just any plan – a plan that is comprehensive, adaptable, and relentless in its pursuit of excellence.

As you delve deeper, you'll come to understand the significance of identifying and connecting with your target audience. You will explore the science of consumer behavior and discover how knowing your ideal customer is like having the key to unlock their hearts and wallets. Customer insights will be your North Star in this marketing voyage, guiding you towards tailored solutions that resonate with your audience's desires.

In the world of business, you're never alone; you're surrounded by competitors, both known and unknown. This book will arm you with the knowledge and strategies to not only survive but thrive amidst the rivals, illuminating the paths to victory and revealing the snares that lie in wait.

The concept of a Unique selling Proposition (USP) will be your guiding principle. It's the beacon that separates your business from the crowd, signaling why you are the better choice. Through strategic positioning, you'll learn to shape how your brand is perceived, anchoring it in the hearts and minds of your customers.

But remember, marketing is not merely about spending; it's about investing. Every marketing action should contribute to your Return on Investment (ROI). In this book, I'll teach you to make informed decisions that optimize ROI, maximizing the returns on your marketing endeavors.

However, as you traverse this marketing landscape, You must acknowledge that change is the only constant. A successful marketing plan is adaptable, responsive to evolving market dynamics, and open to feedback. The marketplace is dynamic, and your marketing plan must be agile.

Moreover, as you embark on this journey, do so with ethics and legality as your unwavering companions. This book emphasizes the importance of conducting business with integrity, ensuring that your marketing practices align with legal requirements and industry ethical standards.

The chapters to follow will be your treasured guides, each unlocking a new dimension of marketing mastery. As you prepare to dive into the heart of this book, remember that your business isn't just a venture; it's a legacy in the making.

Get ready, dear reader, to embark on a journey that will empower you to acquire new customers, boost your profits, and emerge as a prominent figure in your industry. This is your roadmap to marketing excellence, and the destination is nothing less than enduring success.

So, turn the page and let the adventure begin.

Chapter 1

What is the marketing plan?

A marketing plan is a detailed document that lays out advertising and marketing strategies for the upcoming year. It outlines specific marketing objectives and the associated business activities within a defined timeframe. This plan includes an assessment of the current marketing position, a discussion about the target market, and an explanation of the marketing strategies used to achieve these objectives. While it follows a formal structure, it's adaptable for use as either a formal or informal reference. The marketing plan encompasses historical data, future predictions, and methods for reaching marketing objectives. It typically begins with market research to identify customer needs and how the business can meet these needs while ensuring a satisfactory return on investment. This process involves market analysis, action plans, budgeting, sales forecasts, strategies, and projected financial statements. Essentially, a marketing plan acts as a tool to help a business make optimal use of its resources to attain corporate goals. It may also conduct a comprehensive analysis of the company's strengths and weaknesses, its organizational structure, and its products.

The marketing plan outlines the specific steps and actions required to achieve its objectives. For instance, it might include a strategy to increase a business's market share by fifteen percent, along with the associated goals to accomplish this growth. This plan serves to describe how a company will utilize its marketing resources to meet its marketing objectives. Marketing planning also involves segmenting markets, defining market positions, forecasting market size, and planning for a feasible market share within each market segment. Additionally, it can be used to create a detailed case for introducing a new product, revamping existing marketing strategies, or incorporating a company marketing plan into the corporate or business strategy..

The why and when of planning

Marketing planning directs the team toward achieving meaningful outcomes that support specific marketing initiatives and the overall company objectives. It ensures that all customer-facing teams are aligned and that activities are in sync with broader goals by connecting programs and campaigns to the marketing strategy.

The timing and frequency of planning can vary among companies. Many marketing teams focus on programs and campaigns for the next six months or even annually. Others opt for quarterly planning that aligns with the organization's business cycles. The key is to start the process early to allow ample time to address all aspects of planning.

One of the primary purposes of developing a marketing plan is to set the company on a specific marketing path. Marketing goals typically align with broader company objectives, and the plan outlines how these goals will be achieved. For instance, a new company aiming for growth may emphasize strategies to expand its customer base, which often requires systematic talent acquisition.

When creating a Marketing Plan and conducting Market Research, two approaches can be taken: internal and external. Internal research focuses on improving the experience and products for existing customers, while external research seeks to attract new customers.

Marketing planning encompasses objectives like gaining market share, increasing customer awareness, and enhancing the company's image. It also outlines the required budget and resources to achieve the plan's goals. The marketing plan provides a roadmap for what the company aims to achieve within the budget, allowing company executives to evaluate the potential return on their marketing investment. Various aspects of the marketing plan involve accountability.

The marketing plan is a shared responsibility of company leaders and the marketing team to steer the company in a specific direction. After strategies are defined and tasks are developed, each task is assigned to individuals or teams for implementation. These assigned roles enable companies to track milestones and communicate with teams during the implementation process. The marketing plan serves as a blueprint to achieve organizational goals, guiding the path to objectives. Having a marketing plan helps company leaders monitor and develop their functional areas, like increasing sales staff to boost sales if that's a marketing plan goal.

The marketing plan fosters productive discussions between employees and organizational leaders, promoting good communication within the company. It also allows the marketing team to analyze past decisions and results, aiding in better preparation for the future. It provides the opportunity to observe and study the operating environment.

An action plan ensures that, in the long run, a company can assess and monitor the success of its approaches, particularly regarding the introduction of a new brand. However, the importance of the business team is often overlooked. Businesses require qualified personnel to deliver the services and products customers demand. High-caliber employees enable the business to operate smoothly and expand in line with strategic plan objectives. This may involve a diverse group, including those in the insurance sector and support personnel in marketing and IT. Implementing a recruitment solution can streamline and simplify the hiring process, enhancing quality, accuracy, and consistency. Automating hiring benefits the organization's talent pool and the productivity of hired staff. It helps reduce the cost of hiring top talent and expedites the hiring process to meet strategic growth and revenue development goals.

First time entrepreneur and beginner marketer mistake

Many small business owners and new entrepreneurs often assume that creating a superior product or offering an exceptional service will naturally attract their target market. This assumption has its merits since people have needs and actively seek to fulfill them. However, while this logic is sound, it can lead to significant marketing errors. The challenge people face in the modern, developed world is not finding ways to meet their needs, but rather dealing with an overwhelming array of choices to meet those needs. We are inundated with options, and even if your product or service is exceptional or objectively the best, it won't be chosen if it's not visible and memorable enough for people to seek it out.

This is precisely why marketing plays a pivotal role in a business's success – it's the tool that enables you to break through the flood of choices and establish a lasting presence in people's minds. Nonetheless, it's surprising how many small businesses and startups falter in their marketing efforts. To prevent you from making these common mistakes, we've put together a concise list of the marketing errors we frequently observe.

Mistake 1. Not Making Marketing a Priority

The most significant error made by small business owners in marketing is simply not engaging in it. While this might initially sound surprising, it becomes understandable when we consider the myriad of responsibilities entrepreneurs, especially those who are just starting, have on their plate. They are preoccupied with the quest for top-quality products or services, building a high-caliber team, mastering effective delegation, securing startup funding, and budget planning. Although it's crucial for businesses to inform people about what they offer, it's no wonder that owners often end up neglecting marketing as they are deeply engrossed in creating and financing their offerings.

What's more, it's not enough for business owners to merely recognize the importance of marketing to avoid falling into this trap. Take, for example, Justine Leconte, a fashion vlogger and entrepreneur with a reputation for her ethically sourced fashion line and adept use of social media. She is a business owner who clearly understands her customer base and has a well-defined brand tailored to those customers. Yet, when it comes to effective marketing, even Leconte concedes that she's not immune to its challenges. She recently shared some of the mistakes she made when starting her business, one of which was not dedicating sufficient time to marketing. In her video, you can see her cringe as she admits that her intense focus on acquiring quality products caused her to miss many opportunities to promote her new line. The surprising twist is that Leconte's professional background is in...marketing. Her regrets underscore how easy it is to become overwhelmed by the various aspects of running a small business and highlight how significant a mistake this can be. Leconte herself suggests that at least 50% of a business owner's workload should be allocated to marketing if they are handling it themselves.

Mistake 2. Not Building a Website

Once again, in the digital age, this may appear to be an unthinkable oversight, but research reveals that it is a common one. According to SCORE, a non-profit organization, only 51% of businesses have websites. While word-of-mouth and traditional marketing methods like signage and print materials are still essential, the reality is that even when consumers search for local products and services, 96% of them turn to online searches, as reported by Forbes Magazine. So, not having a website is akin to not having a door on your business, effectively forcing potential customers to crawl through a window. While they may be interested in what you offer, they won't go to the trouble of crawling through a window. As a result, you miss out on numerous potential customers, which, in turn, means missing out on potential revenue.

Although some small business owners may genuinely believe that having a website is unimportant, for most of us, the reason for neglecting website creation is the same as our general marketing neglect: a) uncertainty about how to do it, and b) being too busy to invest the time in figuring it out. However, it is absolutely imperative to have a digital presence for your business.

Mistake 3. Failing to create an EFFECTIVE Website.

Often, businesses will go as far as building a website, but that website might have a cumbersome handle, requiring a bit of jiggling and a hard push to open. This is what we typically refer to as an informational website – it's good for displaying your location, business hours, and services. However, if your website's sole purpose is to provide information, you're not fully harnessing its potential. After all, if you've gone through the effort of creating a website, it should be working hard to persuade customers to make a purchase. Hence, websites should be optimized for conversion, not merely serving as information repositories. According to Neil Patel, businesses with websites designed for conversion are "twice as likely to experience a substantial increase in sales."

Designing for conversion involves considering several factors. For instance, it's crucial to make your value proposition immediately clear within the first 0-8 seconds, convincing your audience that you have what they desire, and it's exclusive. Other critical aspects include creating compelling calls to action and headlines, as well as crafting content that narrates a story and establishes social proof. Effective web design goes beyond aesthetics and providing information; those aspects alone are insufficient to drive conversions.

Constructing an exceptional website is undoubtedly challenging, but the rewards can be substantial. After creating and testing your website to effectively target your audience, you can potentially boost your conversion rates by up to 300%.

Mistake 4. Lacking the Knowledge to Collect Marketing Data (And Apply It).

If you lack the means to evaluate your marketing's reach, how can you ensure that you're reaching anyone at all, let alone the right individuals who genuinely care about your product or service? In reality, you can't.

You might believe that you lack the resources, whether in terms of time or money, to monitor and analyze how your marketing is engaging with the audience.

Yet, the reason tracking and leveraging this data is so crucial is precisely because small businesses cannot afford to waste resources. If you can't pinpoint where your marketing is falling short and rectify the problem, or if you're investing in marketing to people uninterested in your offerings, you're essentially squandering valuable resources. Given a limited marketing budget, it's essential to ensure that every penny is employed effectively.

Numerous software tools are available for discovering and monitoring leads. However, to optimize their effectiveness, these tools must be employed strategically, and this demands a fundamental understanding of how marketing functions in general. Some small business owners possess this understanding, while others lack it, which leads to the next common mistake...

Mistake 5: Overlooking Foundational Marketing Research

Chances are, you're an expert in the product or service your business offers to the public. You might be an exceptional chef, a bicycle craftsman since childhood, or an individual who dedicated ten years to becoming a lawyer. Such expertise didn't manifest overnight; it resulted from hard work, practice, and self-education in your field.

Surprisingly, many experts like you, embarking on entrepreneurial ventures, attempt to manage their own marketing without even cracking open a marketing book. If you intend to handle your own marketing, you need to educate yourself about marketing strategies, techniques, and theories just as thoroughly as you educated yourself about your area of expertise as a business owner. If you're here, you've already begun exploring the available information, which is commendable. However, it's only the tip of the iceberg. Before commencing your small business, you should read at least three or four books about marketing and internalize the knowledge. Anything by Seth Godin is an excellent starting point—his books are concise, straightforward, and easy to grasp.

After conducting your research, you'll need to formulate a written marketing strategy, much like the written business plan you've created. Numerous guides and templates are available to assist you in this process. Nevertheless, the task of drafting this strategy is not merely a fill-in-the-blank exercise. Your plan must be custom-tailored to work optimally for your business, which requires a substantial investment of time and thought into its creation and how you'll employ it to guide your marketing decisions.

Mistake 6: Failing to Set a Realistic Marketing Budget

If all of this is beginning to seem somewhat overwhelming, there's a good reason for that. Marketing is demanding work, and there's a great deal riding on its success. As mentioned earlier, Justine Leconte advised small business owners to allocate 50% of their efforts as startup entrepreneurs to marketing. While this isn't hard data, it is consistent with the time and energy that successful small business owners report dedicating to marketing.

However, what if you can't allocate 50%? You're not alone in this predicament. Most of us cannot dedicate 50% of our time and energy to marketing because our businesses demand our attention. At some point, we all need to allocate time for sleeping, eating, and perhaps engaging with our loved ones. In such cases, outsourcing your marketing efforts should be considered.

Outsourcing offers a dual benefit. First, you reclaim 50% of your time and energy for other crucial tasks. Second, a reputable marketing agency is likely to perform a more effective job in marketing your business because they are experts with extensive experience. Even if you've self-educated in marketing and read several books, it won't match the level of expertise, not to mention the manpower, that a marketing agency can provide.

Gene Marks, the owner of the successful tech consulting firm The Marks Group PC, often emphasizes the significance of delegation in his interviews and speeches. He states that one of his success secrets is delegation. When he began hiring individuals to handle specific tasks because he couldn't manage everything, he learned that he shouldn't manage everything, even if he could. In essence, he was handling tasks at which he wasn't particularly skilled. His advice is clear: "Focus on what you do best, and delegate the rest."

Developing an Effective Marketing Plan

When formulating your marketing plan, you must start with two fundamental elements: understanding your business identity and comprehending your customers. Examine your business critically to identify the central products and solutions that define your mission. Another crucial step is to assess the effectiveness of your existing marketing efforts. What is working well, and what isn't? You might be surprised to discover that you're not as familiar with your business as you assumed. A candid examination of your business's actual status is essential to create a solid, effective marketing plan.

Next, it's imperative to gain a deep understanding of your customers. Who are the individuals you are currently reaching? Are they the customers you need and desire? Identifying your target customer will help you shape your marketing plan effectively, regardless of their demographic variations.

Lastly, understanding your competition is essential. Examine other businesses in your industry, analyze their marketing strategies, and evaluate their customer following. What are they doing that you're not? What are you doing that they aren't? Identify areas of overlap. These comparative analyses will provide valuable insights into what elements should be included in your content marketing plan.

Conduct Comprehensive Research

Don't solely rely on your initial impressions and intuition when evaluating your business and customers. First impressions can often be misleading. Data is your most valuable tool, and scrutinizing the data to understand what people are genuinely engaging with (as opposed to what you assume they're engaging with) will be foundational in creating your content marketing plan. Online behavior is another critical area to explore. What are people searching for, and how can your

Diversify Your Approach

When crafting your marketing plan, it's essential to explore two distinct areas, each with its set of four key elements.

Consider the four primary marketing strategies:

1. Cause marketing: Linking a company and its products/services to a social cause or issue.

2. Relationship marketing: Focused on strengthening the bond between your customer and your business.

3. Scarcity marketing: Creating a perception of limited availability to encourage swift customer purchases.

4. Undercover marketing: Employing subtle methods to market to customers without them realizing they are being marketed to.

It's important to keep in mind the principle of marketing mix while formulating and devising your content marketing plan. Often referred to as the "4P's," these components encompass product (or

service), place, price, and promotion.
Maintaining a diverse mix of these
different content types is essential to keep
your marketing approach fresh and
engaging for your customers.

Evaluate and Adjust Your Marketing Plan

An effective marketing plan is one that's
perpetually evolving. It's not a one-time,
fixed strategy. Ideally, you should
consistently assess and adapt your plan to
maintain its effectiveness and alignment
with your brand. Instead of the saying
"adapt or die," think of it as "adapt and
THRIVE." Regard your marketing plan as
a living, ever-changing document to help

you generate revenue and achieve your objectives.

Chapter 2

Selecting your target market

Think of your target market as a way to focus your marketing efforts on segments more likely to make purchases. Target marketing is a more efficient, effective, and cost-effective approach to reach customers and generate business. It represents a subset of the total market.

It's crucial to distinguish between the target market and the target audience. The target audience is narrower, referring to the consumers you expect to buy the product. This audience may or may not overlap with the target market. For instance, a children's toy may have a target market of boys aged 6 to 12, but it's the parents (who actually make the purchase) who form the target audience.

The target market comprises individuals with similar needs, perceptions, and interests who tend to favor the same brands and respond similarly to market changes. Meanwhile, the target audience consists of individuals with comparable expectations from organizations or marketers.

For instance, individuals globally looking to reduce their calorie intake represent the target market for a product like Kellogg's K Special, which promises weight loss in two weeks. Conversely, those who sweat more may be more interested in purchasing perfumes and deodorants with a long-lasting fragrance.

Selecting the Target Market

Organizations or marketers must identify the specific group of people they wish to target. This involves understanding the needs and expectations of these individuals.

Key steps in selecting a target market include:

1. Identifying similar characteristics among individuals.

2. Grouping individuals with shared characteristics to create a target market within a broader market.

3. Analyzing factors such as lifestyle, age, income, spending capacity, education, profession, gender, mentality, social status, and environment.

It's essential to remember that trying to appeal to everyone will not lead to success; being specific in targeting is crucial.

Let's consider the example of soap usage. While the product is the same, people use it for various reasons, such as combating body odor, fighting germs, obtaining fairer skin, or achieving a younger-looking complexion. These differing needs result in different target audiences:

- Target Audience A: Those using soap to combat body odor, which may include marketing professionals, sales representatives, and individuals exposed to prolonged sun exposure or public transport.

- Target Audience B: Those using soap to fight germs and infections, which could encompass individuals working in healthcare or unhygienic conditions.

- Target Audience C: Those aiming for fairer skin, often teenagers and college students.

- Target Audience D: Those desiring a younger-looking complexion, typically individuals aged 30-50 or older.

External factors like climate and geographical location also play a role in defining the target market, as deodorants and perfumes sell better in humid and warm regions.

Crafting your message

In the ever-evolving realm of modern marketing, it's increasingly evident that one of the most vital factors for success is skillful communication. To captivate and motivate their intended audience, businesses must craft messages that profoundly connect with them. In pages that follow, I will delve into the essential components of effective marketing communication and offer insights on how businesses can create messages that genuinely engage their audience.

Comprehending Your Audience

The initial step in crafting effective marketing communication is gaining a profound understanding of your audience. This involves examining their demographics, psychographics, and behaviors to gain insights into their motivations and desires. It necessitates thorough research, careful analysis, and a readiness to listen and respond to feedback. By comprehending your audience's needs, desires, and preferences, you can shape messages that truly resonate with them, making them feel acknowledged and understood.

People are more likely to connect with a message that speaks directly to them. When your message resonates with your audience, they're more inclined to respond to your call to action, share your message, or provide feedback. They are also more likely to trust you and consider you an authority in your industry. By demonstrating your understanding of their challenges and your capacity to offer solutions, you can build a robust relationship with your audience, steering their purchasing decisions.

Crafting a Captivating Brand Narrative

To authentically connect with your audience, you must construct a compelling brand story that addresses their deepest desires and aspirations. This necessitates a profound grasp of your brand's values, mission, and unique selling proposition, as well as a willingness to be authentic and transparent in your messaging. By creating a brand story that profoundly resonates with your audience, you can forge a powerful emotional connection that fosters engagement and loyalty. In today's crowded marketplace, differentiation is essential to stand out from the competition. A distinctive brand story helps distinguish a company and form a memorable identity. It assures consistency in messaging across all marketing channels. When a brand story is consistently conveyed, it reinforces the brand's identity and message, making it more memorable and recognizable.

Developing a Consistent Brand Voice

Effective marketing communication necessitates a consistent brand voice that spans all channels and interactions. This entails shaping a lucid and consistent messaging strategy and investing in high-quality content that mirrors your brand's values and character. By establishing a strong brand voice, you can generate a sense of continuity and familiarity that nurtures trust and bolsters credibility among your audience.

A uniform brand voice across all communication channels, encompassing social media, email, advertising, and customer service, aids in establishing a unified brand image and enhancing brand recognition. Furthermore, a robust brand voice allows businesses to construct an emotional link with their intended audience. By employing language and messaging that resonates with their customers' values, emotions, and aspirations, businesses can nurture trust and loyalty, resulting in repeat business and positive word-of-mouth recommendations.

Forging Emotional Bonds

At the core of effective marketing communication is the aptitude to foster emotional connections with your audience. This requires profound insights into human psychology and the factors that drive emotional engagement, such as storytelling, humor, and empathy. By crafting messages that speak to your audience's emotions, you can form a potent bond that cultivates loyalty and advocacy.

Emotional connections can set a brand apart from its rivals. In today's saturated marketplace, standing out can be challenging. By developing emotional connections with consumers, brands can differentiate themselves and create a unique identity that resonates with consumers. When consumers feel a robust emotional connection to a brand, they are more inclined to engage with the brand's content and share it with their social circles. This can lead to increased brand awareness, reach, and sales.

Measuring and Enhancing Outcomes

Finally, it's crucial to gauge and refine the results of your marketing communication endeavors. This involves meticulous tracking and analysis of key performance indicators, as well as a readiness to experiment and iterate based on the insights gained. By consistently refining your messaging strategy, you can craft messages that genuinely resonate with your audience and produce tangible results.

Effective marketing communication demands a profound understanding of your audience, a captivating brand narrative, a strong brand voice, emotional connections, and a willingness to gauge and enhance results. By investing in these essential components, businesses can create messages that authentically connect with their audience, stimulating engagement, loyalty, and growth.

Reaching Prospects Using Advertising Tools

Advertising often remains one of the most misunderstood and costly aspects of the marketing process. Frequently, I find myself in conversations with business owners who:

1. Lack clarity on the effectiveness of their marketing efforts.

2. Rely exclusively on a single medium to reach their target audience.

3. Manage prospect nurturing manually.

Do you recognize your situation in this description? I'm not suggesting you're entirely off course. Nevertheless, I believe there's a more effective path, one that involves understanding what good advertising entails and how to harness the right media strategies.

So, let's delve into the common misconceptions surrounding advertising media and share valuable insights to optimize your investments.

What Constitutes Effective Advertising?

Many businesses aspire to achieve widespread media exposure, whether it's through billboards, TV commercials, print publications, or online channels. The allure of broad recognition is undeniable. However, here's the challenge: Your target audience is likely at home, streaming content on platforms like Netflix. Squandering your budget on media channels that your prospects don't engage with is detrimental to both your business and bank account.

While it might feel satisfying to announce, "I've been featured in prestigious publications like Forbes or The New York Times," this may often be more about stroking your ego. The real objective is to generate revenue discreetly, a strategy that has proven effective for me.

I'm confident that 99.99% of the global population is unaware of my existence, and that's perfectly fine with me. I don't mind it, as long as the remaining 0.01% constitutes my target audience, people who recognize me, connect with me, and engage in business with me.

So, what defines effective advertising?

It's not about spreading your name to the widest possible audience; it's about connecting with the right audience and motivating them to choose your product or service. Achieving this requires a crystal-clear understanding of your audience and what drives them.

Track Your Metrics

From a marketing perspective, it's crucial to adopt a "money at a discount" mindset. Consider this perspective: you are essentially purchasing customers. To ensure profitability, you should acquire them at a lower cost than what they bring in through purchases.

What would you be willing to pay for a prospect who could potentially yield

$10,000 or $100,000 in revenue? Estimating this figure is challenging until you start tracking your metrics.

Regardless of the advertising media you use, there are essential metrics to monitor:

1. **Leads:** How many leads have you generated?

2. **Conversion Rate:** What percentage of these leads decided to make a purchase?

3. **Cost of Customer Acquisition:** How much did you spend to acquire a customer or client?

4. **Average Transaction Value (front-end):** Calculated by dividing the total sales value by the number of sales.

5. **Lifetime Value (back-end):** The average amount a customer spends on your business over their entire engagement period.

The first two metrics are relatively straightforward, but you should also be familiar with the terms "front-end" and "back-end."

Front-end refers to a customer's initial purchase stemming from your advertising efforts, while back-end encompasses subsequent purchases, often through subscriptions or ongoing services. The ideal scenario is to profit both in the front-end and back-end. While incurring an initial loss in the front-end isn't unusual, the goal is to secure an upfront return on investment.

Your metrics will fluctuate over time, either increasing or decreasing. Even slight changes in these numbers can significantly impact your overall results. This underscores the importance of diligent metric tracking. Relying on estimates is insufficient; you need precise data to assess the efficacy of your media platforms.

Avoid Sole Dependency on a Single Source

Relying solely on one platform for lead generation can be risky. Placing all your trust in a single platform, be it Google, Facebook, or Amazon, can be precarious. A single negative incident could result in the suspension of your account, leading to the loss of your entire following without a means of contact.

While having a primary platform can be advantageous, diversifying your media channels is prudent. I recommend using at least five different media platforms to establish connections, advertise, generate leads, and earn revenue. For instance, media pitching can secure free press for your business and contribute to lead generation.

For those new to marketing, it's beneficial to strike a balance between digital and offline media. These aren't as complex as they may seem. Here's a breakdown:

Digital Media:

- Digital media is effective for building your opt-in list and expanding your customer base. Your website serves as a key digital asset that drives business growth.

- You have multiple opportunities for opt-ins, whether on your home page, product pages, or blog site.

- Utilize various digital platforms, including social media (Facebook, Twitter, Instagram, LinkedIn), media sharing platforms (TikTok, YouTube, Spotify), e-commerce platforms (Amazon, eBay, AliExpress, Etsy), and public relations through content contributions and press releases.

Offline Media (Traditional Channels):

- Offline media, reminiscent of traditional advertising, can still benefit your business.

This encompasses radio, television, billboards, and direct mail (snail mail).

- Offline media isn't obsolete, and it can capture audience attention effectively.

Considering the effectiveness of both digital and offline media, adopting a multimedia approach is advisable. This involves focusing on media platforms where you can maintain ongoing connections with your audience.

Hire Experts

Advertising media often constitutes the most expensive component of your marketing strategy, serving as the bridge between you and your target market. A common mistake is attempting to manage everything on your own, akin to herding cats. If you're unsure about a particular aspect, hiring experts is a prudent approach.

Running a business can be likened to a team sport. When you lack expertise in certain areas, it's sensible to engage someone skilled in that domain. If you're unfamiliar with how Facebook Ads work, consider hiring a Facebook ads expert. If crafting the perfect email for email marketing eludes you, bring in an email marketing specialist, and so on.

In a team sport, you require different skills within the team. Here's the strategy:

1. List the media platforms you intend to use for your marketing, ensuring your target audience is active on these platforms.

2. Engage specialists to enhance your team's competence.

3. Incorporate these specialists into your in-house team.

Use a Variety of Tools

No single all-in-one tool can fulfill all your marketing requirements. Although some attempts exist, they often fall short compared to specialized tools. An array of specialized tools is more practical than relying on a single, all-encompassing tool.

Consider hiring a carpenter to construct shelves for your room. You would expect this carpenter to arrive with a toolbox containing a range of specialized tools. A single, all-in-one tool might raise doubts about the carpenter's professionalism.

Similarly, your media strategy necessitates a range of tools for tasks such as team communication, payment processing, customer relationship management (CRM), and more. Here are five tools I recommend:

1. Team Communication:

- G-suite

- Slack

- Zoom

These tools are essential, especially if your business operates virtually. They facilitate efficient communication for both small and large teams. Separate tools for team meetings, like Zoom, are also necessary.

2. Calendar and Scheduling:

- Google Calendar

- Calendly

Google Calendar offers a clear overview of your schedule, simplifying team coordination. Calendly streamlines scheduling by allowing individuals to book appointments based

3. Customer Relationship Management (CRM) Solutions

Consider CRM systems like Ontraport, ActiveCampaign, and ConvertKit. When evaluating these systems, focus on their ability to assist in capturing opt-ins from your website. Look for CRMs that offer segmentation, automation capabilities, and the capacity to free up your time for more critical tasks.

4. Online Training Platforms

Utilize online training and webinar tools such as Zoom Webinars, GoToWebinar, and Vimeo. For instance, I host a weekly webinar using Zoom Webinars, which records sessions in high definition and features advanced functionalities like Q&A sessions and polling. Keep an eye on alternatives like GoToWebinar and Vimeo, as online training and webinars are potent tools for converting leads within the middle of the sales funnel.

5. Payment Processing Solutions

Choose from payment channels like ThriveCart, SamCart, Shopify, Magento, and WooCommerce. My personal preference is ThriveCart, but competitive options like SamCart are worth exploring. If your business operates in the e-commerce sector, platforms like Shopify, Magento, or WooCommerce might suit your needs.

Regardless of the system you select, ensure it integrates seamlessly with your CRM. This integration is crucial; for instance, when a customer makes a purchase, you should be able to identify them as a buyer. This eliminates the need to send prospect-style emails to customers who have already made a purchase. Additionally, prioritize a straightforward and user-friendly interface for payment processing, avoiding extraneous fields and processes that complicate the payment experience. The aim is to ensure a smooth and efficient payment process for everyone.

Chapter 3

Capturing leads

Reluctance to make purchases from unfamiliar businesses is a sentiment both you and your customers share. To address this, it's essential to establish an efficient procedure for gathering the contact details of potential customers. This approach allows you to cultivate trust, showcase your offerings, and eventually transform your site visitors into paying clientele.

Lead capture, in essence, is the process of acquiring personal contact details from prospective leads, with the goal of converting them into loyal, paying customers down the line. It is a valuable marketing tactic that should be an integral component of any comprehensive strategy.

You might be pondering the significance of lead capture and what it entails. Lead capture involves the solicitation of personal contact information, such as names and email addresses, from individuals visiting your website or social media platforms. This information helps build a repository of potential leads that can be contacted in the future with tailored offers designed to entice them into making a purchase from your business.

By accumulating personal data from potential buyers and website visitors, you gain valuable insights into your target audience and start to establish enduring relationships with your client base founded on loyalty and trust. The key to success lies in offering potential leads something of sufficient value to encourage them to willingly share their contact details. This could be in the form of a complimentary ebook, discounts, or a free demonstration.

When executed effectively, lead capture serves as a valuable marketing asset, particularly when you consider that, on average, only approximately 30% of visitors will return to your website. By collecting their personal data, you can nurture relationships with potential leads and persuade them to come back.

Now, how to capture leads? There are various methods presently used for obtaining lead information. For instance, you can employ lead capture forms for activities like newsletter subscriptions or requests for quotes on your website. Additionally, you may choose to use pop-ups or virtual chatbots to gather personal data from site visitors.

Regardless of the method you select, it's crucial to keep in mind the three fundamental principles of lead capture:

- Clearly define the purpose and objectives of each lead capture campaign.
- Ensure you offer something valuable to potential leads so they are willing to exchange their contact information in return.
- Avoid requesting an excessive amount of personal information—an email address is typically sufficient. Striking the right balance between giving and receiving is key to success in this endeavor.

Nurturing leads

Nurturing leads within the realm of marketing is an indispensable process involving the cultivation and maintenance of relationships with potential customers. This practice holds particular importance in today's marketing landscape, where customers possess a higher level of knowledge and discernment than ever before. Here are key considerations to take into account:

1. **Understanding Leads:** Effective lead nurturing commences with a comprehensive comprehension of your leads. You must gain insights into their preferences, pain points, and their position

within their purchasing journey. This segmentation empowers you to tailor your messages to resonate effectively with them.

2. **Content Strategy:** The foundation of lead nurturing lies in furnishing valuable content. Craft content that addresses your leads' inquiries and worries, directing them toward a solution. This content can encompass blog posts, ebooks, webinars, and more.

3. **Multi-Channel Approach:** Harness various marketing channels to engage your leads where they frequent. This encompasses email marketing, social

media, and even personalized direct mail. Maintaining a consistent message across these channels is imperative.

4. **Lead Scoring:** Implement a lead scoring mechanism to identify the most promising leads. This allows you to prioritize your efforts and concentrate on the leads with the highest potential for conversion.

5. **Marketing Automation:** The utilization of marketing automation tools can significantly enhance lead nurturing. These tools enable you to dispatch personalized and timely messages based

on lead behavior, resulting in time-saving and heightened efficiency.

6. **Personalization:** Customize your communication to cater to the specific requirements of each lead. People value messages that appear tailored to their needs rather than generic.

7. **Feedback Loops:** Foster and collect feedback from leads to continuously refine your nurturing strategies.

8. **Measure and Optimize:** Keep tabs on the efficacy of your lead nurturing endeavors. Metrics like conversion rates, open rates, and click-through rates serve as indicators of success. Leverage this data

to fine-tune your strategies as time progresses.

In a world where the buyer's journey often follows a non-linear path, and consumers face an abundance of choices, effective lead nurturing can serve as the distinguishing factor between missed opportunities and loyal customers. It's all about constructing trust, delivering value, and guiding leads along their route to becoming loyal customers.

Sales conversion

The term is quite straightforward and essentially defines itself. Sales conversion refers to the process of turning a prospect into a lead and subsequently converting that lead into a customer. To grasp this concept, it's important to familiarize ourselves with several related terms:

Elements of Sales Conversion

1) Prospects: A prospect is a potential future customer who expresses interest in your product or service. However, a prospect may or may not evolve into a lead, and if not managed effectively, that prospect may be lost or even convert to a competitor. Prospects are the initial stage of the sales process and require persistent pursuit. Nonetheless, communication with prospects should be introductory and non-intrusive, rather than overwhelming.

Gentle communication is less likely to deter prospects, and over time, prospects tend to transform into leads.

2) Leads: A lead represents a promising prospect who has agreed to consider becoming a customer. However, it is the responsibility of the salesperson to nurture the lead and guide them toward making a purchase. Effectively communicating with leads and conducting sales interactions aimed at addressing customer needs and desires is crucial. Aggressively pursuing leads is essential to convert them into customers.

3) New Customer: A new customer is an individual who has never purchased the company's products or services before. If the customer was previously using competing products and then switches to your products, it's referred to as a competitor conversion. It may also happen that the customer is entirely new to the market and has not used competitor products, in which case some may call them a "Fresh Customer."

4) Competitor Conversion: When a customer transitions from using products or services offered by competitors to using your products, it's termed a competitor conversion. Keeping a close watch on how many conversions are attributed to competitors' sales activities and the competitors' sales conversion rates is important.

5) Customer Upgrade: A customer upgrade takes place when a customer shifts from basic products to premium products within the same company. This is also known as a higher conversion. Some companies may categorize this as either a fresh conversion or consider the customer as a new customer for that specific product.

Sales conversion can encompass new customers, existing customers who upgrade to higher-value segments, or competitor sales conversions. Regardless of the scenario, customers should be followed up with from the prospect stage all the way through to conversion. This process of conversion is commonly referred to as the "Sales Funnel."

Process of Sales Conversion

The Sales Funnel is an effective tool for understanding the sales conversion process. It involves converting a prospect into a customer by sifting through the entire population and following a structured process. The steps in the Sales conversion process are as follows:

- **Awareness:** As the name suggests, the target population needs to be made aware of the seller's products. This can be achieved through various media channels. Without raising awareness, the population will remain uninformed about the offerings, and without awareness, there will be no sales. Hence, making customers aware through advertisements or other communication methods is crucial.

- **Interest:** The second stage of Sales Conversion is generating interest. Those who express interest after becoming aware engage in this stage.

In certain industries, salespersons must generate interest by asking appropriate closed-ended questions. It's important at this stage to use closed-ended questions rather than open-ended questions, as this stage determines whether the prospect should be followed up with or not. Closed-ended questions during a sales call or in an interest form allow the seller to clearly understand the customer's intentions.

- **Decision Making:** This stage puts the skills of the salesperson into action. Effective opening of the sales call, setting clear objectives, promptly addressing any customer doubts, and providing product demonstrations are essential tasks for the salesperson. Convincing skills are of paramount importance at this stage since the decision hinges on whether the lead will be converted into a customer.

- **Action:** If the decision is positive, the sale occurs, and if it's negative, the lead will be lost or considered a cold lead. The action stage is where the decision turns into actual behavior.

Example of Sales Conversion

Let's walk through this process with an example. Imagine you're scrolling through social media and come across an advertisement for the new iPad Pro 12.9 inch. You click on the ad, watch it, but eventually close it, thinking the product is too expensive. At the end of the ad, there's a survey form related to the advertisement that you complete, and it also asks for your contact information.

Later, you receive a call from the Apple store, inquiring if you recently viewed their ad, and you confirm that you did. This is when you transition into a prospect. The Apple store invites you to visit at a specified time to learn more about their offers, to which you agree. This is the interest stage. You go to the store and have a conversation with a sales expert who elaborates on the features and benefits of the product. Finally, they present you with a flexible financing option, which helps you overcome the price hurdle.

This marks the decision-making stage, where you agree to make the purchase. As part of the action, you make the initial payment, and the sale is completed. If you were previously using a Microsoft Surface and switched to an iPad, it would be considered a competitor conversion. However, if you had never used a tablet before, it would be classified as a new sales conversion. By progressing through these stages, it's possible to convert prospects and guide them down the sales funnel to achieve sales conversion.

Chapter 4

Unique selling proposition

A Unique Selling Proposition (USP) pertains to the distinctive advantage demonstrated by a company, service, product, or brand, which distinguishes it from its competitors. This unique selling proposition should emphasize product benefits that hold significance for consumers. The USP revolves around clear statements of distinctiveness, backed by objectively verifiable product attributes or practical benefits.

1. Every advertisement should present a clear offer to the consumer, not mere empty words, exaggerated

product claims, or superficial display advertising. Each advertisement should convey to every reader: "Purchase this product for this distinct advantage."

2. This proposition must be something that sets it apart from what the competition can or does provide. It must be exceptional, whether it's related to the brand or a statement that other advertising in the same field doesn't make.

3. Furthermore, the proposition must be compelling enough to not only retain existing customers but also draw in new ones, reaching a broad audience

that includes both current and potential customers.

The USP concept is now one of the eight primary creative approaches used in advertising. The USP approach is recommended when a product category is characterized by high levels of technological innovation. A clear USP helps consumers discern differences, even when there may not be any substantial distinctions, between various brand offerings in a category. It also aids in shaping a positive brand perception and can contribute to improved brand recall.

To determine a suitable USP for a brand, marketers need to conduct extensive research within the category and among consumers. It's crucial to identify a niche in the market, ensure that the feature is unique and valuable to potential customers. Marketers should also put themselves in the customer's shoes and be passionate and confident about the product's potential for success. Having a unique selling point before selling can be advantageous. Being distinct in the market is a significant advantage as it draws customers to a business that offers something no one else does, whether those differences are subtle or pronounced.

In markets with many similar products, using a USP is a campaign method to differentiate the product from the competition. Products or services without differentiation risk being perceived as commodities, which can lead to price competition. A unique selling point is vital for a business to succeed in competitive markets with potential new entrants.

For instance, in the desktop personal computer market, Apple used the slogan "Beauty outside, Beast inside" to differentiate its Mac Pro as a visually appealing product compared to other desktop computers. This approach allowed Apple to charge a premium price.

Wal-Mart, on the other hand, focuses on being the most affordable department store, emphasizing that the price of a product isn't what matters. Such a straightforward message that highlights the business's unique selling proposition can attract customers.

A good USP should target a specific audience and deliver on its promises to establish trustworthiness.

Effective unique selling points differentiate a product or brand from the competition in a compelling way, motivating customers to explore the offering further and consider other aspects of the company's messaging. Check the products below:

- Canva: Empowering people worldwide to create stunning designs. Canva is an online graphic design tool that streamlines the design process for users of all backgrounds. Its USP conveys a platform known for its user-friendliness and broad appeal, emphasizing that it's simpler to use than competing products.
- Hiut Denim Co.: Excelling in one specialty. Unlike many firms, Hiut Denim specializes solely in crafting jeans. Rather than concealing this

fact, the brand leverages it in its marketing. The USP implies that this company excels at what it does because it concentrates exclusively on one area and is less likely to get sidetracked compared to competitors.

- Patagonia: Dedicated to preserving our planet. Patagonia positions itself not just as a clothing retailer but as a brand with a mission. The USP distinguishes the brand while resonating with environmentally-conscious customers who seek to make responsible choices with their purchases.

- Peet's Coffee: The original coffee craftsmanship. The first Peet's coffee shop opened in 1966, sparking a coffee revolution that continues to influence the industry today. Peet's USP capitalizes on its history, setting it apart from other coffee vendors and highlighting its unmatched experience and expertise.

- Shopify: The foundation of e-commerce. Shopify is a leading e-commerce platform that provides tools for online merchandise sales. Millions of businesses across 175 countries rely on this service. Shopify's USP emphasizes its dominant position in the market, widespread popularity, and overall user-friendliness, guiding customers to the right platform for their needs.

To the prospective Customer's question, Your USP is your answer

In the realm of marketing, the Unique Selling Proposition (USP) serves as the definitive reply to a potential customer's inquiry. It's the remedy for their doubts, the antidote to their uncertainties, and the guiding light that assists them in making a decision.

When a prospective customer inquiries, "Why should I select your product or service?" or "What makes you different from the competition?" your USP steps up as the succinct, compelling solution. It encapsulates the distinct value you offer, clearly explaining why your offering stands out as the superior choice.

Your USP not only addresses their reservations but also instills confidence. It showcases your expertise, underscores your commitment to delivering a personalized solution, and underscores the genuine value your product or service brings to their life or business.

In a crowded market with abundant choices, your USP sets you apart from the crowd. It spotlights the advantages that make your offering a standout choice, resolving issues, and proactively addressing pain points.

Ultimately, your USP is the persuasive force that draws potential customers nearer to becoming loyal supporters. It's the response that motivates them to take action, whether it's making a purchase, requesting a demo, or deepening their engagement with your brand.

Consistency and clarity are pivotal—your USP should be consistently communicated through all touchpoints, ensuring that each time a prospective customer seeks answers, they receive the same, lucid message regarding what makes your offering unique.

Your USP is the compass that guides potential customers through a sea of options, objections, and uncertainties. It's the guiding star that illuminates the path to a decision, bringing them closer to the realization that your product or service aligns best with their needs and desires.

Chapter 5

Implementation issues in marketing planning

Executing a marketing plan is a critical phase within the strategic process, and it brings about its own distinct set of obstacles. These challenges during the implementation phase can significantly influence the triumph of your marketing endeavors.

Harmonizing the marketing plan with the broader organizational strategy stands out as a primary concern in marketing planning implementation. Ensuring that the marketing plan aligns with the overall goals and objectives of the organization can prove to be intricate, particularly within larger or decentralized entities.

Efficient allocation of resources and prudent budget management are also pivotal issues. It is imperative to allocate resources effectively for the execution of the marketing plan, encompassing budget distribution, personnel, technology, and other essential assets. Challenges may arise when juggling these resources against competing priorities.

Team collaboration is of utmost importance, and effective communication is fundamental for seamless execution. Discord within the marketing team or between various departments can lead to inconsistent messaging and efforts, which can affect the overall campaign's success.

Additional challenges emerge from the dynamics of the market and competition. Market conditions can undergo rapid changes, which may impact the effectiveness of the plan. Flexibility and responsiveness to shifts in the competitive landscape are necessary for sustaining a competitive edge.

Tracking and evaluating the plan's performance can pose complexities. The establishment of clear key performance indicators (KPIs) and the monitoring of progress are vital, but collecting and interpreting data can be challenging, especially in the rapidly evolving landscape of digital marketing.

Compliance with regulatory and legal requirements is another prominent concern. Marketing efforts must adhere to various regulations, which can vary by region and industry. Navigating this intricate terrain while maintaining marketing effectiveness necessitates careful attention.

Lastly, ensuring consistency across diverse marketing channels and touchpoints is paramount. A unified brand message and experience are essential for building trust and loyalty with customers.

The effective implementation of a marketing plan calls for a strategic approach that addresses these issues, aligns with broader company goals, optimizes resource allocation, fosters collaboration, remains adaptable in a changing landscape, upholds regulatory compliance, and delivers a consistent brand experience. Tackling these challenges can substantially enhance the effectiveness of your marketing efforts.

Measuring the Effectiveness of Marketing Planning

Evaluating the effectiveness of marketing planning is a vital component of any marketing strategy. It furnishes valuable insights into the success of your endeavors and identifies areas for improvement. Several key factors play a pivotal role in this process.

First and foremost, the most conspicuous metric for gauging the effectiveness of marketing planning is the return on investment (ROI). This metric quantifies the financial gains relative to the resources and funds invested in the marketing plan. A positive ROI denotes a successful plan, while a negative ROI calls for reevaluation.

Monitoring key performance indicators (KPIs) is another critical aspect. KPIs can vary based on the specific objectives of your marketing plan but may encompass metrics like conversion rates, website traffic, customer acquisition cost, and customer lifetime value. Analyzing these metrics provides a comprehensive view of your plan's performance.

Customer feedback and satisfaction are equally crucial. Gathering customer input through surveys, reviews, and direct communication offers valuable insights into how your marketing plan is perceived and whether it resonates with your target audience.

Competitive analysis is yet another method to assess the effectiveness of marketing planning. By comparing your performance to that of your competitors, you can gain a clearer perspective on your strengths and weaknesses.

Brand awareness and recognition metrics, such as brand recall and customer loyalty, are fundamental for evaluating how effectively your marketing plan is contributing to the establishment and reinforcement of your brand in the minds of consumers.

Moreover, tracking the consistency of messaging and brand presentation across different channels and touchpoints ensures that your marketing plan aligns with your brand's image and values.

Measuring the effectiveness of marketing planning entails a multifaceted approach. It encompasses financial metrics like ROI, performance KPIs, customer feedback, competitive analysis, brand recognition, and message consistency. A comprehensive assessment of these factors is essential for comprehending the impact and success of your marketing strategies.

Conclusion

In the closing Page of "Marketing Plan for Business Growth: Acquire New Customers, Boost Profits, and Standing Tall in the Crowd," we find ourselves at the crossroads of transformation and achievement. This journey through the intricacies of marketing strategy, the pursuit of new customer acquisitions, and the relentless pursuit of increased profits has been nothing short of a thrilling adventure.

As we conclude this journey, we're left with a profound understanding that effective marketing isn't just a business necessity; it's the beating heart of sustainable growth. Your marketing plan, meticulously crafted and executed, serves as a powerful catalyst, propelling your business to unparalleled heights in a fiercely competitive landscape.

The pages of this book have been your guiding stars in this marketing odyssey, offering insights into crafting clear and actionable objectives. You've learned how to pinpoint your ideal audience, creating connections that resonate deeply with their needs and desires. Through meticulous competitive analysis, you've identified opportunities and threats, enabling you to carve out a unique space in the market.

The concept of a Unique Value Proposition (UVP) has resonated throughout, reminding us that, in a crowded marketplace, your distinctiveness is your superpower. You've explored the nuances of strategic positioning, meticulously shaping how your brand is perceived, and what it represents in the minds of your customers.

This book has advocated a relentless focus on ROI, driving home the message that every marketing action should be a strategic investment in the growth of your business. Yet, flexibility has also been stressed; for as we know, the only constant in the world of marketing is change.

Adaptation is not just a choice but a necessity.

And what's more, the world of marketing extends far beyond digital platforms and advertising. It encompasses a commitment to ethics and legality, ensuring that your business operates with integrity.

As you prepare to embark on the next leg of your marketing journey, remember that a marketing plan is not a static document. It is a living, breathing guide that must evolve with your business and the ever-changing marketplace. Keep your eye on the horizon and be open to feedback, for it is in the dialogue with your customers that the most precious insights are found.

In conclusion, the book "Marketing Plan for Business Growth" has armed you with the knowledge, tools, and mindset to conquer the market, acquire new customers, boost your profits, and stand tall amidst the crowd. The world of business is not for the faint-hearted, but with a well-crafted marketing plan, it becomes an arena where you can thrive, excel, and become a shining star. Go forth, dear reader, and let your marketing brilliance illuminate your path to enduring success.